TESTIMONY

TESTIMONY

J.R. DAVIS

This work of poetry is dedicated to God.
It is my testimony so far, my life, my joys,
my waste, my blessings, and my limitations.
Like my very breath it is all HIS.

Praise the Lord of the Heavens!
For He alone is worthy of our praise!

Laying in her own filth,
her thoughts wonder,
what is this place,
this new vast expanse.
A nursing babe, she desires milk.
She needs it to grow. She seeks more.

This bright new world...

Its like nothing she's witnessed.

Cold and unwelcoming,
she seeks warmth from that which she came.

"Hold me"

She seeks...

Comfort.
Protection.
Cherishing.

This is her first taste of loneliness.
Crying, she pleads to be held.

The soul within her is unclean,
pursuing only that which profits her fleshly aspirations.

Her soul so young will soon discover,

Whatever it seeks will fail.

No meeting of its own ambitions.

Blissfulness never quite grasped.

She sits, she waits.
What else can she do?
Dear God, please hear her cry, she needs you. Selah.

Blurring moments...
Blur.
Blur.
Blur.
Blur.
Blur.
Blur.
Blur.
Blur.

Clarity arrives.

A smile upon her face
Swinging she finds a simple pleasure in the wind against her cheeks.
Back and forth.
Back and forth.
She smiles...such simplicity.
The wind is cool, the sun is warm, she shivers.
Curiosity leads her to release the rope from both hands.
She falls,
Pain is found within.
A consequence of her foolishness.

Arms reach for her, she feels safe.
Comfort.
Security.
Her tears wiped away.
Cheeks caressed.
Scrambling down, unwisely trotting off.

Time mangled.
Life blurs again.
Blur.
Blur.
Blur.

Forgetful in her youth she is foolish,
unaware of her idiocy.
Seeking her own happiness,
ignoring you in your splendidness.
Selah.

Oh, but joy dear King,
Lord of the heavens it seems that she has sought you out of her own selfish desire.
Fearing pain of death and fire,
she begs you for the first time.
Lovingly you affirm her,
receiving her as your daughter.
All of heaven rejoices!

Joy!
Joy!
Joy!

Praise to God!

Holy! Holy! Holy! is the Lord God almighty!

Praise be to the heavens she is found; she cries out to you.

Seeking your face, she begs you, Lord.
She illuminates her friends of your splendor shouting of your goodness.
Oh Lord you are good!
She tells them of you, and your goodness.
Yet they are smug, questioning fools. They make themselves gods.
Her joy falls.
Why, she cannot understand their doubt.
Though soon
she will, her trials await....

Protect her YAHWEH!

She seeks you; she begs for you!!

Begging, Begging, she prays.

Yahweh!
Yahweh!

Help her, she is falling, Lord God Heal her!!

The enemy awaits, he prowls, he strikes and takes her.
Heal!
Heal!
Your power is mighty, oh creator heal her!

Lord God, they cry out to you!! "Heal her, we beg!"
Why.
Why.
WHY!!!
.
.
.
.
.

Why are you allowing this God?

She calls...

for you,
for mercy,
for liberation,
for joy,
for help.

Her pain cries out.
You hear.
You speak.

Yet….
she does not hear,
nor does she want to listen.

Crying to you she asks,

Why God, why?

She cannot see you.
Your answer falls on her deafening ears.
Seeking only after herself, revealing yet again she is but a fool.

Bitter,
time blurs again.
Blur.
Blur.
Blur.

Forgive the fool she is.
She lusts for the things of the flesh.
Longing for another, to be noticed, touched, a jezebel lost in the waves.
She tosses herself amongst the waves of her mind.

The enemy lurks.
seeking...

Pride.
Lust.
Indecency.
Recognition.
Satisfaction.
Egotistical desires.
LIES!
Everything she seeks for her fulfillment fails.

Seeking her flesh,

She wanders.

She reads but does not understand,
she speaks but nothing is uttered,
she wins yet is still at a loss.
Nothing brings her joy.
A foolish fawn she wanders away from you, forgetting,

She repeats the same toil.
Demons feed on her foolish heart.
Without you she is nothing.
She perceives nothing, A fool she remains.
She seeks her flesh.
Call her wretched, in her sorrow she drowns.
She begs your forgiveness,
then she turns back to her filth.
Instead of seeking your glory,
she falls deeper into her sin.
Purposefully missing the mark.
She does not flee; she seeks after death.
Begging for fulfillment.
Her soul wonders down a path of tormenting shame.
Seeking its own.
Rebelling against your spirit....

Repeating what she knows will not bring her joy.
Imitating her past
Foolish, is she?
Oh, the pain!
Her Shame shackles her in her ways.
Immorality holding her down.
Not understanding that her heart must be transformed,
she replicates yet again.
And again, and again.
All of heaven cries...
What a fool!!!

She has humiliated herself, disgraced her father.
Shamed her.
Mother.
Shame.
Shame.
It's all she feels.

In your temple, she looks down.
Embarrassed of her indignity.
Lower than the worms, she again begs.

Oh, it seems she has at last repented!
Crying out,
My God, My God! Take my soul, save me, forgive me!
Make me new!
Older, but still young.
Wiser, but still a fool.
She asks to be made new.

Praising.
Seeking.
Loving.

She finds you dear Lord, yet again.
Like a wayward child you welcome her.

Hearing her prayer, you reach out,
Guiding her to your will.

She steps forward, but temptation lurks.
Pulling away, unaware, she hasn't let go of the chains.
They hold her down.
Her heart waivers.
Speaking to you Lord, she says
"I know but lord just give me your grace tomorrow."

Oh, How long will she play the fool dear God!!??
What a pit she has fallen into.

WOE TO HER!!!

How foolish she is thinking that by choosing her flesh, grace will come.
That no consequences will result of her satisfying the flesh.
It can never be satisfied.
Only for a moment.
Then crawling to the surface
again, it begs...

More.
More
More.
More

The adversary whispers "You've failed, your worthless, I'm all you have."

Foolishly turning to her flesh, she asks,

"Where are you, My GOD!"

Lord, you cannot look upon her...

Not her flesh,
nor her sin,
her pit of hell.

Her wavering heart.
Unfaithful
She wonders.
Seeking desperate desires.
Seeking that which is wind.

Will she ever learn God?

Only you, Yahweh will satisfy the empty hole of her soul.

Only you God can make her whole.

She cries out.
Tears burn her face.

.
.
.
.
.
.
.
.

Tangled in a web of lies from the enemy.
Her despair brings her back to you.

Fleeing, yet seeking.
Longing she finds you.

You have not forsaken her.
Like a wayward child, you delight in her return.
She is the prodigal, received with open arms.
Yet her shame lingers.
Like a blank page, waiting for ink, it stares.

Knowing she will fail again, you hold her, giving grace.
Always waiting for her return.

She asks... where are you God?
I cannot see you!
I cannot touch you!
I cannot feel YOU!
Yet I need you!
I do not understand, show me your face!
She demands of you as if a child. She is foolish.

But dear God, you are so patient,
So kind, and you whisper,

"I am here" ....

Oh, what a blessing, you have given her a mate!
A companion
For this difficult journey.
Her soul cries for him,
Two souls, bound by God.

Sanctify him She cries!!
She prays.
She waits.
She Prays.
She waits.
And again, you hear her.
you respond to her cry.

Unsure of the blessing you have bestowed.

She fears.
The enemy lingers.
Hoping to devour.

She does not see it, nor does her lover.
How she loves him.
Her companion.
He does not waiver.
Seeing him is pleasant.
His touch like mead.
Strong. Sweat. Healthy in moderation.
What joy!
His company,
Fleeting.
Oh, what blessing to find friendship in your lover!

Oh, but she stumbles.
Foolishly she neglects.
Seeking self.
Fresh torment awaits.
An invitation from her foes.

She seeks the wrong things.
Believing the enemy's lies.
Faltering.
Longing makes way for fear.
Fear for longing
Is she enough?
Self-doubt makes room for loneliness.
And loneliness for temptation...

Her adversary murmurs,
"Don't worry, I'm still here."

Confused.
Forgetful.
Hurt.

She stumbles...
Seeking the enemy instead of fleeing!
Oh, what a fool!

Desperate she cries out,
"Oh, My Lord !!! How foolish am I.
Giving in to such an obvious invitation and lies from the adversary.
Deliver me from My foes Yahweh!
I am wrought with shame !!"
He hears her cry.
Forgiving her he speaks life.
Reminding her who she is...

His Child.

Nothing Else matters.

Remembering this she pushes forward.

Her lover holds her.
He strokes her hair.
Oh, how foolish we've been my love!
But we are one and God is our refuge.
He speaks life.
Leading his lover
But her foolish heart doesn't hear.
Pride setting in. Ignorance takes root. For now, it goes unnoticed.

.

.

.

.

.

She cries!!
"Oh, what Joy Lord!
What a blessed day it is!
You have blessed my womb.
Praise be to you!

Oh, my Lord!
NO NO NO!!!
It cannot be.

Where God
Where is the blessing?
You've taken it!
But why?
What have I done to anger you, my Lord?!

Am I a fool?

Please Yahweh I beg save my child from this terrible thing.
I cannot bear the pain!
Please breath life back into him!"

As a fool yet again she seeks herself,

"Oh lord what joy, you can hear my cry!
Praise be again!

Oh, but why do you keep teasing my womb,
Tearing from me what is mine!
What have I Done!

Where oh God are my children!
I beg of you!
Please hold them for me.
Promise me oh God!
I cannot bear it!
I need to hold them!
They are mine, oh dear God!
WHY OH WHY?
My heart, my soul has never felt such anguish!!!
Dear God, WHY!"

Her heart aching.
She picked up the pieces.
She tried to forget and move forward.

Oh Lord.
She loves you but knows not her place.
Teach her Lord!
Questioning the creator of the universe, her bitterness swells.
Who is she to question you?
Knowing best.
Knowing all.
Only you can understand it.
She is but a fool, still unknowingly seeking her flesh.
Not you, but herself.
Will she ever learn.
What a fool she is.
Her thoughts are foolish.
Questioning her existence, her purpose, she hurts.

Yet you find her.

Her joy and pain will lead her to you yet again.
Oh, Yahweh you are so good!

Knowing all,
Giving great blessing!
Her womb, it overflows.
Oh, what joy!
But wait,
Such joy it brings great pain.
Confused she seeks you.
Oh lord the adversary will not win this time. In her pain seeking you she praises.
You are her living water.
You are her joy.
Bringing praises to you, she is content just being in your presence.

What a wonderful gift, oh my lord how grateful am I!
But how can I care for such a small being?
I cannot sleep.
I am afraid.
What if I fail?
What if my child dies?
What if I hurt them?
What if I am not good enough?
Lies!
What Lies!
The enemy torments my mind!
I will not listen!
The enemy waits, I will not wander.
For you have made me for this purpose.
Forgive my wandering heart oh LORD!
What joy you have given me.
They are your children.
I must care for them.
They are a great blessing!

Though she is still a fool
Some wisdom has been gained.

In her pain she praises you.
The enemy kept at bay.

Holy Holy HOLY are you LORD!!

On occasion
Her heart wonders,
seeking contentment in worldly things...
Always failing...
like the fool she is ...
Looking up to you she asks, "will I ever learn"?

Help me!
Oh, my lord, help me to seek after you and nothing else!
Give me comfort oh my LORD, I beg it of you!

Help Me!
It is to much, so difficult, I cannot continue.
Oh my God!
Why did you not tell me?
How selfish I am!
Show me, through these little blessings,
SHOW ME how to sacrifice!!!

I am convicted.
I am such a fool, seeking myself always.
Woe, what pain is this! Oh lord please forgive me!
I want to serve them, love them, cherish them!

But oh, my flesh fights, tormenting my soul, the enemy waits.
Culture yelling....
Pursue self!
Selfish ambition!
Do what's best for you!
Be selfish!

Are you happy?

Comparison

Creating discontentment.

Discontentment stealing my joy.

Oh, what a vicious cycle.

What LIES! The enemy is a fool.

My hope rests in you!
My joy is not of this world but in you!
I am a child of the highest!
You are my GOD, and I am your child!
The enemy trembles at your name!
I ask them by who's authority they are here, with your name they are cast away!
you are my protecter and my God!
I will not fear, as I feel their breath down my neck.
The battle has already been won!
What can be done to me?
Nothing!!!

Yeshua, you are king!!!
AMEN! and AMEN!

Her Prayer...

I am nothing.
I offer you nothing my God.
Why do you bless me?
Giving me breath, knowing I will only waste it?
Why do you give me bread, knowing I will let it spoil?
I don't want to waste the favors you give.
Oh, dear Lord, help me to multiply your blessings.
I cannot do this alone.
My pride begs me to keep silent, but I cry out to you!
I am selfish in all I do. I seek after my own.
Please make me righteous in your eyes.
Help me. Show me how to hold fast to your ways.
Teach me, make me wise.
Yet again I am a fool.

As a fool, like Eve here I stand seeking knowledge.
Looking back like Ado.
Questioning like Marium.
Attempting to be like you.
Such a fool I am and shall always be.
Wait...show me how to love you Lord, how to seek you, dear God forgive me and my failures. Help me to know you in every moment.
I want to walk with you lord.
Selah.